Veterinarians
help keep animals healthy

Bobbie Kalman

🌳 Crabtree Publishing Company

www.crabtreebooks.com

Created by Bobbie Kalman

Dedicated by Crystal Foxton
To my sweetie John, for always making me smile!

Editor-in-Chief
Bobbie Kalman

Writing team
Bobbie Kalman
Laura Hysert

Substantive editor
Kathryn Smithyman

Project editor
Reagan Miller

Editors
Molly Aloian
Kristina Lundblad
Kelley MacAulay

Art director
Robert MacGregor

Design
Margaret Amy Reiach
Samantha Crabtree (series logo)

Production coordinator
Katherine Kantor

Photo research
Crystal Foxton

Consultant
Michael A. Dutton, DVM, DABVP
Weare Animal Hospital, www.weareanimalhospital.com

Special thanks to
Allan Ivey, Kyle Foxton, Zack Sikkens, Ingrid Sikkens, John Sikkens Jr.,
Alissa Lefebvre, Aimee Lefebvre, Jacquie Lefebvre, Dr. Bruce A. Hunter,
Domenique Davies, Mikell Bering, Bonnie Kozarichuk, Jenny McSpadden,
Dr. Henk ten Oever, Lincoln Animal Clinic, Edgar and Lisa Krick,
Mac Smith, Melba, and Terra

Photographs
Bruce Coleman Inc.: Michael Renner: page 22
Cincinnati Zoo and Botanical Garden: page 23
Marc Crabtree: front cover (people and goats), back cover,
    title page (middle), 3, 4, 5, 6, 8, 9 (top), 10, 11, 12 (top), 13, 15, 16, 17, 19,
    20, 24 (top), 27, 28 (bottom), 29 (bottom), 31 (girl and dog)
Christophe Ratier/NHPA: page 25 (top)
Mac Smith, University of Georgia: page 21
Jim Steinberg/Photo Researchers, Inc.: page 14
©Steve Smith/Superstock: page 18
Visuals Unlimited: William Weber: page 24 (bottom)
©Wolfgang Kaehler, www.wkaehlerphoto.com: page 26
Other images by Digital Stock and Photodisc

Illustrations
Barbara Bedell: border (gorilla, gerbil, frog, and dog)
Antoinette "Cookie" DeBiasi: border (sheep)
Margaret Amy Reiach: border (bird and rabbit), pages 4, 13
Bonna Rouse: pages 7, 26

Crabtree Publishing Company

www.crabtreebooks.com   1-800-387-7650

Cataloging-in-Publication Data
Kalman, Bobbie.
  Veterinarians help keep animals healthy / Bobbie Kalman ; principal
photography by Marc Crabtree.
    p. cm. -- (My community and its helpers series)
  Includes index.
  ISBN 0-7787-2097-7 (RLB) -- ISBN 0-7787-2125-6 (pbk.)
 1. Veterinarians--Juvenile literature. 2. Veterinary medicine--Juvenile
literature. 3. Veterinary medicine--Vocational guidance--Juvenile literature.
I. Crabtree, Marc. II. Title.
  SF756.K25 2004
  636.089'069--dc22
                                                      2004014180
                                                      LC

**Published in
the United States**

PMB16A
350 Fifth Ave.
Suite 3308
New York, NY
10118

**Published
in Canada**

616 Welland Ave.,
St. Catharines, Ontario,
Canada
L2M 5V6

**Published in the
United Kingdom**

73 Lime Walk
Headington
Oxford
OX3 7AD
United Kingdom

**Published
in Australia**

386 Mt. Alexander Rd.,
Ascot Vale (Melbourne)
VIC 3032

Contents

What is a veterinarian?

A **veterinarian** or "vet" is a doctor who **treats**, or cares for, animals that are sick or injured. Veterinarians also **prevent** animals from getting sick. They work hard to help animals stay healthy.

Many types of vets

Different types of vets care for different types of animals. Most vets care mainly for pets. Some vets treat farm animals. Others care for animals that live in zoos. Keep reading to learn more about vets and the types of animals they help.

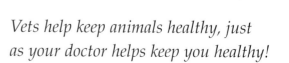

Vets help keep animals healthy, just as your doctor helps keep you healthy!

What is a community?

Vets are **community helpers**. A **community** is an area and the people who live in that area. Community helpers are people who work to keep communities healthy, safe, and fun. Doctors and police officers are community helpers who help people. Communities also have animals that need to stay healthy and safe. Veterinarians treat animals, just as doctors and nurses care for people.

Farm-animal vets help farmers raise healthy animals.

Ready for work

Some vets work indoors, and others work outdoors. Outdoor vets work in all kinds of weather. Wherever vets work, they need to wear clean, comfortable clothing.

Washing hands

Vets often work with many animals each day. Some of the animals are sick. Vets must make sure they do not spread **germs** from one animal to another. They wash their hands before and after they touch an animal.

Covering clothes

Vets who work indoors often wear **lab coats**, or long jackets that protect their clothes. Farm-animal vets wear rubber boots and **coveralls**, shown left, while they work in barns or outdoors in mud.

This farm-animal vet's clothing protects him from dirt and germs that animals might be carrying.

Tools and equipment

Vets **examine**, or look carefully at, the bodies of animals. Vets use many of the same tools and equipment your doctor might use to examine you.

An **otoscope**, shown right, is a tool that has a tiny light. The light helps the vet see inside an animal's ears. Harmful *parasites*, such as ear mites, might live inside an animal's ears!

A vet uses a **stethoscope**, shown left, to listen to an animal's heart and lungs.

(below) A vet uses a **hypodermic syringe** and a needle to give an animal medicine and to take blood from an animal's body.

(below) A vet uses an **ophthalmoscope** to look closely at an animal's eyes.

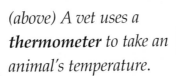

(above) A vet uses a **thermometer** to take an animal's temperature.

Vets for pets

Most vets care for **domestic**, or pet, animals such as cats, dogs, and **rodents**. These vets work at **clinics**, or places where medical care is given. Pets visit vets for regular checkups or when they are sick or injured. Pet owners make appointments for their pets and then take the pets to the clinics.

A veterinarian examines animals to make sure they are healthy. The vet listens to each pet's heart and lungs. The vet also gives pets **vaccines** to protect them from diseases such as **distemper**. Distemper is a dangerous disease that causes animals to lose their appetites and become very sick.

*During a checkup, the vet examines an animal's teeth, ears, eyes, skin, and **coat**, or fur. He also looks for signs of diseases or parasites.*

Learn from a vet

A vet will help you keep your pet healthy. He or she will tell you the best food to give your pet and the amount of food your pet needs. A vet will also explain how to **groom**, or clean, your pet and how much exercise it needs. If your pet needs medicine, a vet will show you how to give the medicine to your pet.

As your pet grows, it may need different types of food to keep it healthy and strong. Ask your vet which kind of food is best for your pet.

An important test

Your pet's examination may include a **blood test**. To do a blood test, the vet takes a small sample of your pet's blood. The blood sample is then sent to a **laboratory**, where it is tested for diseases, such as **heartworm disease**. Heartworm disease can harm your pet's heart. Most vets have small laboratories in their clinics, where they can perform basic medical tests.

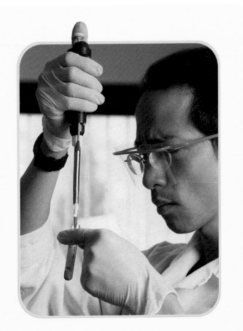

At the clinic

It is important to take your pet to the veterinarian for regular checkups and vaccines. Your pet will probably be nervous in the vet's clinic. You should know what to expect when you go to the clinic so you can comfort your pet. The vet's clinic looks like a doctor's office, but it is a lot noisier!

The waiting room

The **waiting room** is where you and your pet wait to see the veterinarian. Follow the tips below to keep your pet safe and calm while you are in the waiting room:

• Keep your pet on a leash or in a carrier or cage so it will not bother other people or animals.

• Keep your pet away from the other animals in the waiting room. Other pets may have diseases your pet can catch.

• Talk to your pet in a soft voice to help it stay calm.

The examination room

The vet examines your pet in the **examination room**. You are allowed in, too! The vet will ask you questions about how your pet behaves, how much it sleeps, and what it eats. If your pet has been behaving differently than usual, be sure to tell the vet!

After the exam

After the visit, give your pet a treat or toy to reward it for being good during its checkup. If your pet needs medicine, give it the medicine exactly as the vet has shown you. If your pet's illness does not improve, call the vet right away.

The vet will place your pet on a high table, so he or she can examine it easily.

Pet operations

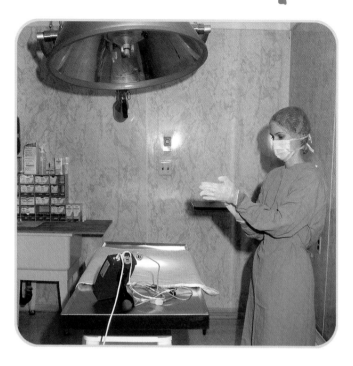

Vets sometimes perform **surgeries**, or operations, on animals. When an animal has a **tumor**, or lump, inside or outside its body, a vet may perform surgery to remove the tumor. If an animal swallows an object, it will need surgery to have the object taken out of its body.

Important surgery

The most common surgeries done on pets are **spaying** and **neutering**. Spaying and neutering stop animals from having babies. Each year, millions of pets are **abandoned**. Abandoned animals are not wanted by their owners and are left outdoors to look after themselves. Unwanted pets are a problem in every community. There are too many pets and not enough people to take care of them! By having your pet spayed or neutered, you are helping to fix this serious problem.

Preparing for surgery

To prepare for surgery, a vet puts on a **surgical gown**, a mask, and **sterile** gloves, as shown on page 12. The vet wears these clothes to prevent germs and dirt from getting inside the animal. Many clinics have **surgery rooms**, where operations take place. Before beginning an operation, the vet gives an animal **anesthesia**. Anesthesia is a medicine that makes an animal sleep through surgery so it will not feel any pain.

Taking x-rays

Most vets have an **x-ray machine** at their clinics. An x-ray machine takes pictures of the inside of an animal's body. X-rays help a vet see if an animal has broken bones or tumors. If an animal swallows an object, the x-ray shows it!

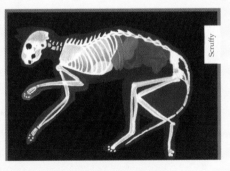

This x-ray clearly shows a cat's bones.

Emergency!

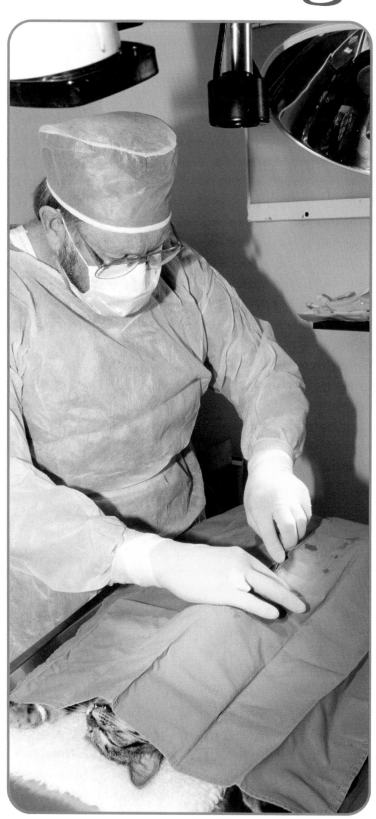

Some vets treat animal **emergencies**. Emergencies are serious events that happen when people do not expect them. The following are examples of emergencies: an animal that has been hit by a car, a female animal that is having trouble giving birth to her babies, or an animal that is vomiting blood.

Day or night

During emergencies, animals do not need appointments. Vets will rush to their clinics, day or night. Vets make sure that time is not wasted because an animal's life may be in danger!

Emergency clinics

Some veterinarians work in animal hospitals or clinics that treat only emergency cases. The vets work at night and on weekends, after most veterinary clinics have closed. Emergency vets know how to treat all kinds of diseases and injuries.

Ready for anything!

Animal hospitals and emergency clinics have surgery rooms and all the equipment that vets need to care for **critically**, or extremely, sick animals.

Special equipment

If an animal needs medicine right away, the vet might put in an **intravenous** or IV. An IV is a tiny needle that goes into an animal's **vein**. Medicine drips through the IV into the vein to make the animal well again. An emergency vet might also use a machine called a **ventilator** to help an injured animal breathe. He or she will check the animal's **heart rate** as well. Heart rate is the number of times a heart beats in one minute.

Healthy heart rates

A vet uses a stethoscope to listen to an animal's heart rate. Some illnesses or injuries can cause heart rates to be much higher or lower than normal heart rates. Vets know the normal heart rates of different animals and can tell if the animals are sick or injured.

When to visit a vet

You can help keep your pet healthy by getting advice from your veterinarian. Ask your vet plenty of questions about how much exercise your pet needs, what to feed your pet, how to groom your pet, and how to care for its ears, teeth, skin, and coat. Knowing a lot about your pet's health can help you keep your pet from getting sick.

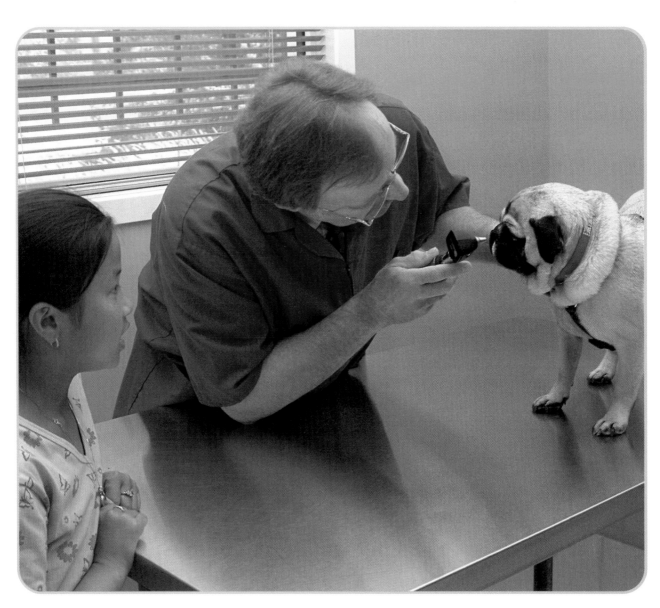

Signs of illness

Sick pets often behave differently than they do when they are well. Take your pet to a vet right away if it shows any signs of illness. Watch for the warning signs listed below.

- Your pet may be sick if it is not eating the usual amount of food or is having difficulty eating or swallowing.

- A sick pet may suddenly gain or lose a lot of weight.

- A sick pet may have trouble breathing.

- If your pet does not feel well, it may drink more or less water than usual.

- Make sure your pet does not have any unusual lumps on its body. Limping and having difficulty getting up or lying down are other signs that your pet needs to visit a vet.

Care in shelters

Animal shelters are places that care for homeless animals. Lost, abandoned, or **abused** pets often end up at animal shelters. An abused animal has been hurt in a serious way by its owner. Animal-shelter vets treat sick or injured animals that are brought to live in shelters.

Many of the animals in an animal shelter are frightened. Animals that have been abused are often scared of people. One important job that animal-shelter vets do is help stop animal abuse. Animal-shelter vets report abuse cases and give the police the **evidence**, or proof, they need to punish the abusers.

The vet gently talks to and cares for all the animals in an animal shelter.

Animals shelters are not **permanent**, or long term, homes for animals. Many of the animals in the shelters are eventually **adopted**. Adopted animals are taken home with people to become their pets. Animal-shelter vets help prepare animals for adoption by spaying or neutering them. The vets give medicines to the animals that have diseases. They also give all the animals in the shelter vaccines to protect them from getting diseases. Animal-shelter vets teach new pet owners how to care for their animals properly.

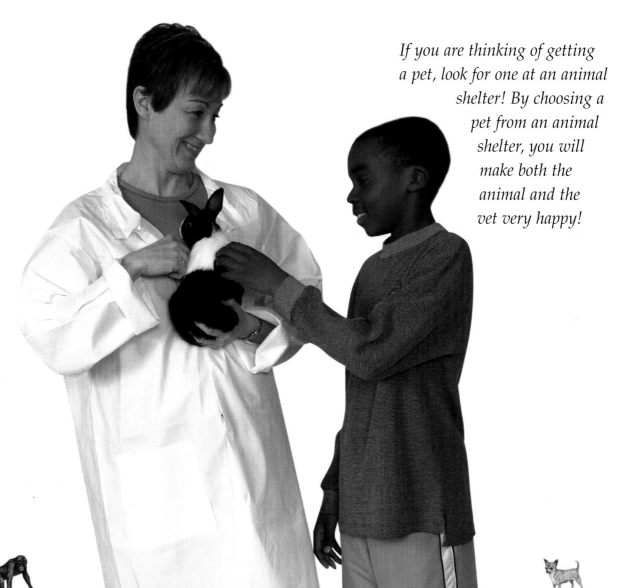

If you are thinking of getting a pet, look for one at an animal shelter! By choosing a pet from an animal shelter, you will make both the animal and the vet very happy!

On the farm

Farm-animal vets drive cars or trucks that carry all the tools and equipment they need.

Farm-animal vets treat farm animals, such as pigs, goats, cattle, and horses. These veterinarians travel from farm to farm, caring for the animals. Farm-animal vets give the animals regular checkups and vaccines. They also handle animal emergencies on farms.

Vets on wheels

A farm-animal vet does not spend much time at a clinic. He or she drives from farm to farm, treating animals in **pens**, **pastures**, and barns. A farm-animal vet may travel as much as 1,000 miles (1609 km) in one week!

A farm-animal vet also teaches people how to care for the animals living on their farms.

Large-animal room

A farm-animal vet sometimes needs to perform surgery on an animal. He or she can perform some surgeries at a farm, but surgeries that require special equipment must be done at a clinic. A farm-animal vet's clinic has a large-animal room, which is used to perform surgeries on big animals. This room has all the equipment the farm-animal vet uses during the surgery.

Heavy lifting!

Before the surgery, the vet gives the animal anesthesia. Once the animal is sleeping, it can be difficult to move! Some vets use **hoists** to move large animals onto an operating table, shown above. A large-animal room usually has a **tilt table**, shown on page 22, which is used for surgery. A tilt table lifts and turns so the vet can work on all the parts of an animal's body.

Wild-animal vets

Wild-animal vets care for animals that live in zoos, **aquariums**, and **nature preserves**. These vets must know a lot about many types of animals! Wild animals in parks, zoos, and on nature preserves live close together.

If one animal gets sick, many others often get sick, as well. They need special care to stay healthy. Wild-animal vets give the animals regular checkups and vaccines. They also make sure the animals eat healthy foods.

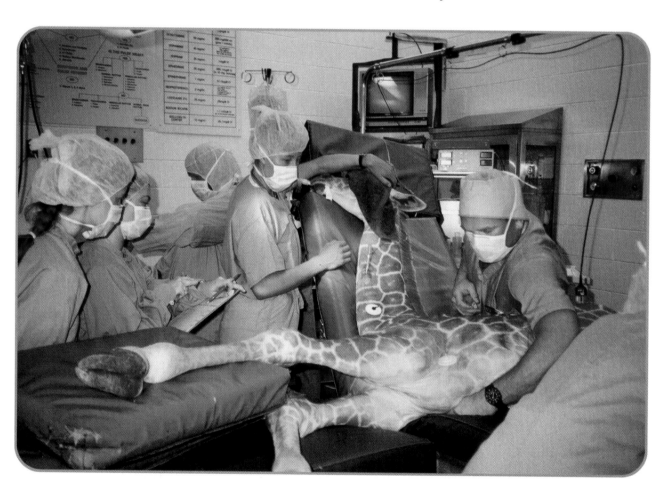

This giraffe is being cared for by a team of wild-animal vets. The vets give the giraffe regular checkups to make sure it stays healthy and strong.

Checkup challenge

Examining wild animals is often a challenge! The only safe way to examine certain animals is to put the animal to sleep first. On nature preserves, wild-animal vets use **blow darts** to put animals to sleep. Blow darts contain anesthesia.

Wild-animal vets blow the darts through a long tube or shoot them from a special gun. Blow darts allow vets to put animals to sleep from a safe distance. Vets must then work quickly to complete the examination before the animal wakes up!

Saving endangered animals

Wild-animal vets also help save **endangered** animals, such as this baby Sumatran rhinoceros. Endangered animals are in danger of dying out in the natural places where they live.

Wild-animal vets help by caring for endangered animals that live in zoos. These vets also teach people why it is important to help save endangered wild animals.

Various vets

There are many other types of veterinarians! Sport-animal vets, **veterinary specialists**, and veterinarian teachers all work hard to help animals and the people who own the animals.

Sport-animal vets

Sport-animal vets treat animals, such as race horses and **rodeo** animals, which are involved in sports. They also treat horses that are used for playing **polo**. Polo is a game played by two teams on horseback. Sport-animal vets care for sport animals with injuries and help these athletic animals stay strong and healthy. They also teach the owners how to care for their animals properly.

Veterinary specialists

A veterinary specialist is a vet who knows a lot about a certain part of an animal's body. Some veterinary specialists are eye doctors, dentists, and vets who treat animals with skin conditions. If your pet has a problem that needs special care, your vet may call on a specialist to help. Wild-animal vets also ask veterinary specialists to help them care for zoo animals.

Teachers and researchers

Many vets are teachers who work at veterinary schools. They teach students who are studying to become veterinarians. Some vets do research to discover new information about animal diseases and to find new ways to help injured animals. Veterinary researchers also study how diseases spread from animals to people. This information helps people in all communities protect themselves against these diseases.

Helping hands

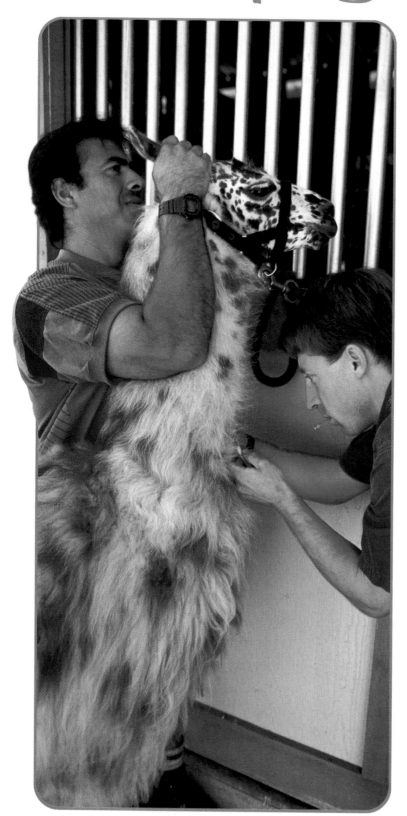

Many veterinarians work with **veterinary assistants**, or people who help vets take care of animals. Veterinary assistants have many jobs to do. They feed, groom, and walk animals that stay at veterinary clinics overnight. Veterinary assistants also help vets treat animals. The veterinary assistant on the left is holding a llama while the vet gives it a needle.

A busy job

Veterinary assistants help vets in many ways. They clean cages and equipment, give animals vaccines, perform x-rays, and assist vets during surgeries.

In some clinics, veterinary assistants help keep records of the treatments given to animals. They also teach owners how to care for their animals.

This veterinary assistant makes sure that the surgery room always has enough supplies. Emergency surgeries can happen at any time!

Becoming a vet

Becoming a vet takes hard work! You must learn and remember a lot of information about many kinds of animals.

Stay in school!

Training to be a vet is similar to training to be a doctor. To become a vet, you must go to school for a long time! The first thing you will need is a high-school diploma. Next, you will study at a college or a university for three or four years. After that, you will have to attend a veterinary college.

These children can learn a lot about animals by helping this farm-animal vet.

School days

At veterinary college, students learn about the bodies of animals. They also learn how to treat animal diseases and injuries. Students get experience working at farms, zoos, and clinics. After graduation, students must pass difficult tests before they can work as vets.

Get experience

If you are interested in becoming a vet, it is a good idea to get experience working with animals. A great way to start is by volunteering at an animal shelter or a veterinary clinic. As a volunteer, you will clean cages and help groom and feed the animals. Doing these jobs will make you feel more comfortable around animals.

Learn more!

You can learn more about veterinarians in your community! Ask your vet questions during your pet's next visit. Take a trip to a zoo and ask the wild-animal vets to tell you how they care for wild animals. Go to the library and read books about vets, animals, and pet care.

This wild-animal vet works at a zoo. He is teaching these children how to care for a snake.

Vets on the web

You can surf the Internet to learn more about vets and animals! Check out these fun websites:

• Care for Animals:
  www.avma.org/careforanimals/

• The Pet Center:
  www.thepetcenter.com

• Animal Doc Com:
  www.uga.edu/~lam/kids/

• Animal Land:
  www.animaland.org

• Kid Territory at the San Diego Zoo:
  www.sandiegozoo.org/kids/

Glossary

Note: Boldfaced words that are defined in the text may not appear in the glossary.

aquarium A place where animals and plants that live in water are displayed to the public

germ A group of tiny cells that can cause diseases

hoist A device used for lifting and moving heavy animals

hypodermic syringe A piece of medical equipment used to inject fluids into the body or draw fluids from the body

laboratory A room or building used for tests, research, and experiments

nature preserve A protected area of land in which several kinds of plants and animals live

parasite A tiny animal living on the skin or inside the body of another animal

pasture A grassy area where animals feed

pen A fenced-in area in which animals live

prevent To keep something from happening

rodents A group of animals with small bodies and sharp front teeth that never stop growing

rodeo A competition in which skills such as riding wild horses or roping calves are displayed

sterile Clean; free from dirt and germs

vaccine A special medicine that helps protect an animal's body from disease

vein A blood vessel in an animal's body that carries blood through the body and to the heart

Index

1 2 3 4 5 6 7 8 9 0 Printed in the U.S.A. 4 3 2 1 0 9 8 7 6 5